The Super Quick Guide to Learning Activities

Sara Miller McCune founded Sage Publishing in 1965 to support the dissemination of usable knowledge and educate a global community. Sage publishes more than 1000 journals and over 800 new books each year, spanning a wide range of subject areas. Our growing selection of library products includes archives, data, case studies and video. Sage remains majority owned by our founder and after her lifetime will become owned by a charitable trust that secures the company's continued independence.

Los Angeles | London | New Delhi | Singapore | Washington DC | Melbourne

The Super Quick Guide to Learning Activities

Andy Goldhawk

Learning Matters
A Sage Publishing Company
1 Oliver's Yard
55 City Road
London EC1Y 1SP

Sage Publications Inc.
2455 Teller Road
Thousand Oaks, California 91320

Sage Publications India Pvt Ltd
B 1/I 1 Mohan Cooperative Industrial Area
Mathura Road
New Delhi 110 044

Sage Publications Asia-Pacific Pte Ltd
3 Church Street
#10-04 Samsung Hub
Singapore 049483

Editor: Amy Thornton
Senior project editor: Chris Marke
Cover design: Wendy Scott
Typeset by: C&M Digitals (P) Ltd, Chennai, India
Printed in the UK

Library of Congress Control Number: 2023941490

British Library Cataloguing in Publication Data

A catalogue record for this book is available from
the British Library.

ISBN 978-1-5296-2970-5
ISBN 978-1-5296-2969-9 (pbk)

At Sage we take sustainability seriously. Most of our products are printed in the UK using responsibly sourced papers
and boards. When we print overseas we ensure sustainable papers are used as measured by the Paper Chain
Project grading system. We undertake an annual audit to monitor our sustainability.

Contents

About the author

Dr Andy Goldhawk was an adult education lecturer for fifteen years. Over this time, he taught English for Speakers of Other Languages (ESOL), Spanish and IT. He has also been a teaching and learning coach. Andy holds a doctorate in education and a master's degree in lifelong learning. He now works at the University of the West of England and lives in North Somerset. This book follows his first, *The Super Quick Guide to Learning Theories and Teaching Approaches*.

Andy is on Instagram at @learning.theories.shared

Acknowledgements

I want to thank Amy Thornton at Sage for supporting my mission for this second book. Thank you to the design team at Sage who have once again produced a vibrant design for the pages in this book. My thanks also to Nicola Goldhawk, Ben Wiggins and Tom Church for your valuable comments, insight and suggestions in reviewing my draft; it is much appreciated. Finally, Nicola, Jude and Remy, for your love, support and encouragement!

Introduction

Thank you for buying this book – I very much hope it is useful to you, whether you are a trainee or experienced teacher, lecturer, early years practitioner, teacher trainer, or anyone else whose work involves planning and facilitating learning activities. The purpose of this book is to provide **nutshell summaries** of over one hundred learning activities, a one-stop introduction and repository of activities that can be understood quickly and adapted as you choose.

There are many differing versions of a learning activity, so the summaries contained within this book are not intended to be definitive or overly prescriptive. As you go, **experiment**, **adapt** and **refine** activities for your subject and your students. Most of the learning activities covered in this book can be characterised as involving **active learning**, meaning that students are doing more than passively listening to the teacher transmit information. An exception to this is the lecture, although, even here, there are some ways to enable students to be active participants (see entry 5.9).

There are various potential approaches to categorising learning activities into chapters. In this book activities are mainly organised by the **principal communication skills** being used in the activity. There is overlap, of course: an activity in the speaking and listening chapter, for instance, does not necessarily mean that it will involve no reading or writing. There is also a chapter on activities that are typically used towards the **start and end of lessons**, and another for activities that tend to be used for **revision** and **assessment**. I recognise that a revision activity might have alternatively been placed within the reading and writing or speaking and listening chapters, this reflecting the multiple features characterising each activity. The Index of entries will, of course, help you navigate your way around. First of all, there's a chapter on **foundational concepts** relating to planning and facilitating learning activities.

For every activity it is important that:

- students understand the **purpose** of a learning activity – for example, that it is introducing or applying new information, rehearsing a skill, enabling discussions about a topic, or assessing that learning has taken place;

- **instructions** are given clearly before the start of any activity, so students understand clearly what they need to do. One way to check students' understanding is to ask them to summarise the instructions back to you or explain the activity in their own words;
- students are given a clear **timeframe** for each activity. On some pages I've suggested indicative timings, but you'll need to experiment, as the time allotted to an activity will need to differ according to factors such as the number of students in a class and what exactly you intend the students to achieve through the activity;
- you are aware of potential **pitfalls** and have **contingencies** in mind;
- you plan how you will support students with different needs, to ensure all students have opportunities to **participate** and are (and feel) a valued member of their group.

The Core Content Framework (CCF)

The learning activities in this book can help trainee educators to develop their teaching practice in relation to various aspects of the Initial Teacher Training Core Content Framework (CCF), particularly:

- 'Classroom Practice' (standard 4: Plan and teach well-structured lessons)
- 'Adaptive Teaching' (standard 5: Adapt teaching)
- 'Assessment' (standard 6: Make accurate and productive use of assessment).

The CCF can be found at: www.gov.uk/government/publications/initial-teacher-training-itt-core-content-framework

Chapter 1

Foundational Concepts

1.1 The Lesson Plan

A **guide** to a period of learning, usually written by the teacher, detailing:

- **what** will be learned in the session (this is articulated in the **learning objectives**, see 1.2);
- the learning **activities** that will help students acquire the knowledge or skills specified in the learning objectives; and
- how learning will be **assessed** (or, demonstrated) and what the required standard is.

Lesson plans may also include **notes** relating to: the previous lesson (such as challenges faced, and the extent to which learning objectives were successfully met); indicative **timings** for each activity; the **materials** needed for the session; how **differentiation** will be incorporated; contingency plans (should an activity not work); and space for **reflections** following the lesson.

1.2 Learning Objectives

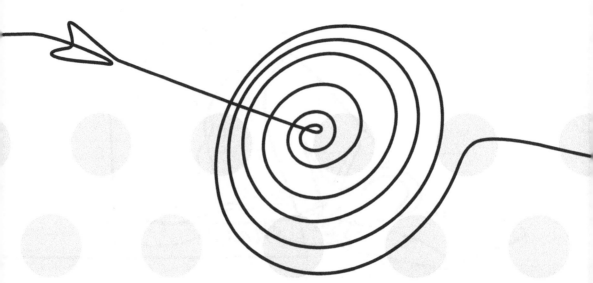

Statements that express the desired **knowledge** or **skills** that students should be able to demonstrate by the end of a lesson, or a longer period of learning. The purpose of most activities in a lesson is to address one or more of these objectives. **Brain breaks**, for example, are an exception (see entry 1.6). Lesson objectives are specific, measurable, and may be differentiated. They are usually shared with students near the start of a lesson and can be revisited at the end, in order that students and the teacher can consider the extent to which objectives have been met, and establish whether further time is needed to achieve the objective. Also see **SMART targets** (entry 1.3).

1.3 SMART Targets

SMART is an acronym for a target that is:

Specific

Measurable

Acceptable/Achievable

Realistic

Time-bound

These features may be used to help articulate learning objectives for a lesson, or targets in individual learning plans.

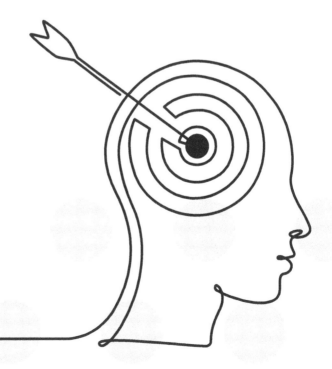

1.4 Realia

Real-world objects that are used to facilitate learning. Students can use different **senses** to interact with these objects to gain an understanding about their characteristics and uses. Examples include a magazine, circuit board, item of clothing, a guitar, or a bouncy ball. Realia is often used in **language teaching** – for instance, to help students **connect** new vocabulary (nouns) with corresponding real-world objects.

1.5 Homework

Learning activities that students complete **outside** of lesson time. Homework can give students opportunities to learn **new** information, **consolidate** prior learning, or can be used to **assess** students' current understanding. Homework can be marked by the teacher, or (with guidance) self-marked, or peer-marked, the latter two options helping students **reflect** on their work (also see **peer marking** 6.5). Homework can help students to practise planning, time management and conscientiousness. However, it may also lead to physical fatigue and negative emotions (see Magalhães et al., 2020, for a useful summary of research on homework).

Magalhães, P., Ferreira, D., Cunha, J. and Rosário, P. (2020) 'Online Vs Traditional Homework: A Systematic Review on the Benefits to Students' Performance', *Computers and Education*, 152, 103869.

1.6 Brain Breaks

Taking place **between** main learning tasks, brain breaks are short activities intended to help rest and re-energise students and aid **memory retention** before the next activity. They can also improve students' **mood** and **engagement**. Brain breaks can be done with students of any age and could involve physical stretches or other movement around the classroom that take as little as **two minutes**.

1.7 Elicitation

The **teacher** draws information from **students** through questioning, rather than immediately providing it to them. Teachers may ask students to describe structure, function, or vocabulary in a language class, for instance. In a vocational context, the teacher might ask students to describe a process, such as how to change a tyre or cut hair to a particular style. This technique therefore recognises students' existing knowledge and experiences relating to a topic and can help teachers diagnose their students' current levels of understanding. Also see **Socratic questions** (1.8), **cold calling** (1.10), and **wait time** (1.11).

1.8 Socratic Questions

This activity involves students coming to knowledge through **questions** and **dialogue**. The teacher asks probing **open-ended** questions and gives students **sufficient time** to process them, and formulate answers (also see **wait time**, 1.11). Key aims of Socratic questions are to explore and question underpinning **beliefs** and **actions**, and stimulate **critical thinking**.

It is important to recognise that some students may not be initially willing to answer questions or engage in dialogues; further, challenging long-held beliefs may create discomfort for some individuals. Also see **cold calling** (1.10).

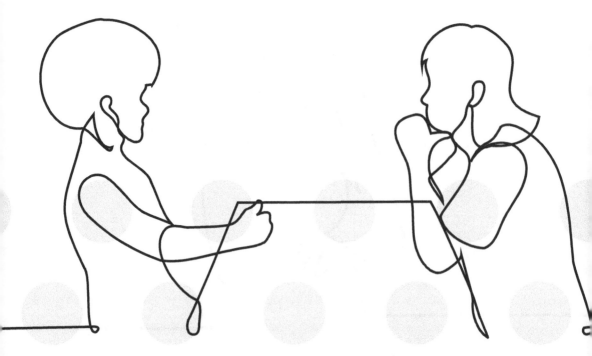

1.9 Hinge Questions

Multiple choice questions asked by the teacher, to help **determine** whether students need to **revisit learning** content (either in part or fully) or are ready to move on to new content. Hinge questions enable teachers to discover important insights as to the **errors** students are currently making in their understanding of a topic. The inclusion of some **plausible** (incorrect) answer options can help the teacher discover whether a student has a partial understanding, or none at all, at that stage.

Obtaining responses from **every student** can be challenging, but strategies such as using **online assessment tools** (see entry 4.12 **online activities 1**) can facilitate the process.

1.10 Cold Calling

The **teacher chooses** students to answer verbal questions, rather than solely taking responses from those with raised hands. This tactic can ensure responses are heard from **all students**, including those not voluntarily offering answers, and thus not only the strongest or most vocal.

Some teachers may avoid this approach to questioning, concerned that some students might feel uncomfortable or humiliated in being required to respond. It has been found, however, that classes involving the consistent use of cold calling leads to the number of students volunteering answers **increasing** over time. Further, students' **comfort levels** in relation to their participation in class discussions have also been found to **improve** (see Dallimore et al., 2013).

Dallimore, E.J., Hertenstein, J.H. and Platt, M.B. (2013) 'Impact of cold-calling on student voluntary participation', *Journal of Management Education*, 37(3), pp. 305–341.

1.11 Wait Time

Moments of silence that are permitted in the time between a teacher's question being posed and a student being selected to respond. Rather than demanding an immediate response, this time enables students to **process** the question, **formulate** a response, and **articulate** their answer. Such time can also help students give more developed or nuanced answers.

Wait time involves around three to five seconds of silence after the question has been posed. Further time can be given after a student's response, in order that others in the group have an opportunity to consider and build on this initial answer.

1.12 Learning Pairs

Students work together in **pairs**. In learning pairs, students can exchange or pool **ideas**, **co-create** work, share work, **critically appraise** their partner's work, or **role-play** (see 3.2). Pairs can also help each other revise with question cards (also see **top trumps**, entry 6.15). The teacher can either let students choose partners or decide themselves. The latter option may be preferred in order to ensure students work with different people and not always with their closest friends.

1.13 Writing Frame

A **template** intended to help students structure sentences and articulate ideas in their writing. Writing frames provide, for example, **sentence starters**, **key words** and/or **connector** words. They may also suggest the order of sections or paragraphs. These items scaffold responses to questions or tasks, and can help students develop an appropriate **writing style** for specific subjects and tasks, such as when explaining a process, or to present opposing arguments.

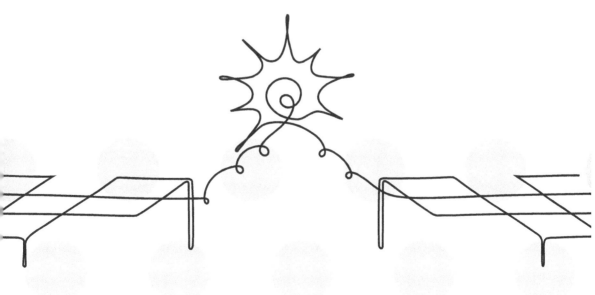

1.14 The Extension

Additional activities that are available to students who complete the main learning task(s) early, fully, and correctly. An extension activity can be used as an opportunity for one or more of the following:

- to reinforce learning
- to enable students to engage in deeper exploration or analysis of the content
- to revise
- to formatively assess learning

Extensions can give students further opportunities to rehearse **higher-order thinking skills**, such as applying what they have learned to a different context, or to solve a problem. Extension activities are not, therefore, simply 'more of the same'.

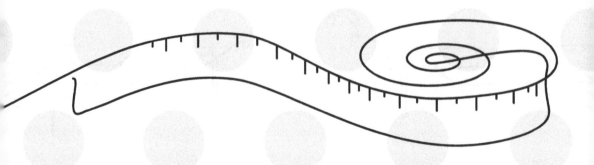

1.15 The Filler

Brief activities such as **word games** and **puzzles** that can be used when students need to be occupied for various reasons, such as when a teacher is **delayed**, or when **covering** a class at the **last minute**. Fillers can also keep faster students usefully occupied when they finish the principal task early, by enabling them to practise or apply new knowledge. Such activities can also facilitate a low-intensity **transition** between main learning activities.

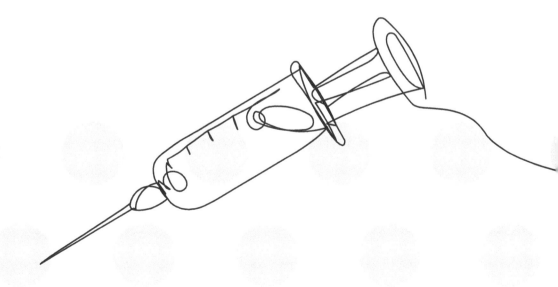

Chapter 2

At the Start and at the End

2.1 The Starter

An activity at the start of a lesson, with one or more of the following purposes:

- to stimulate **recall** of prior learning;
- to **motivate** or **calm** students for upcoming learning;
- to **establish** or **reinforce** routines, rules and expectations;
- to **introduce** new learning content.

Starter activities are wide ranging, and may include a problem-solving task, brain storming (see 2.5) or asking open questions (also see **elicitation**, 1.7).

2.2 Do Now Activity

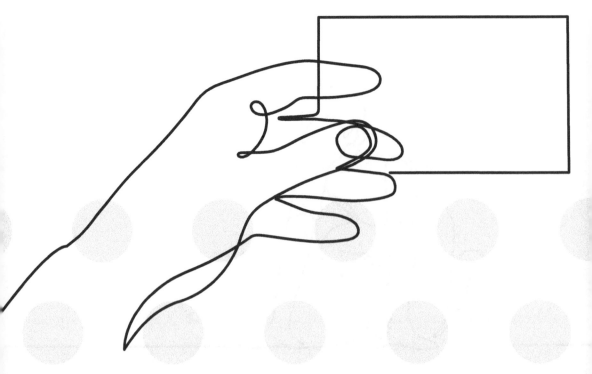

An activity provided at the start of a class that students can do **as soon as they enter** the room. Instructions for a Do Now Activity (or 'DNA') may be displayed on the board, placed on students' desks, or handed to students as they arrive. A DNA might take between five and ten minutes, and can serve to occupy early arriving students and/or introduce the topic of the session. Also see **the starter** (entry 2.1) and **entrance slips** (entry 2.3).

2.3 Entrance Slips

At the **start** of a session, students are given a slip containing one or more questions about a topic, and a few minutes to **write** responses. In doing so the entrance slips encourage students to recall current knowledge, either newly acquired from a previous session or **existing knowledge** students have before instruction.

The teacher can then use what is written to inform how they proceed with the lesson, such as going over previously taught content again to address commonly held misunderstandings. Also see **do now activities** (2.2) and **exit slips** (2.9).

2.4 The Ice Breaker

Ice breakers are usually intended to help students learn each other's names and become better acquainted. Such activities also provide an early opportunity for the teacher to see students 'in action' (speaking and interacting with others).

They can additionally facilitate teambuilding and help introduce a new topic. Example ice breaker games include **speed dating** (see 2.6) or **'two truths and a lie'**. In this latter example, students first circulate, find a partner and introduce themselves. They then take turns to give three facts about themselves, with the partner guessing which is the lie. Students then move on to find a new partner.

2.5 Brainstorming

Aimed at stimulating thinking and creativity, students **generate ideas** relating to a topic, on their own or in groups. Brainstorms may also be used to **encourage recall** of existing knowledge. The focus is usually on producing a large **quantity** of initial ideas, while criticism and judgement of these ideas is withheld until a later stage of evaluation. Pen and paper can be used, or online applications such as **Padlet** or **Mural** (see **online activities** 1, entry 4.12). Students can also be encouraged to **make connections** and **combine** ideas while they brainstorm.

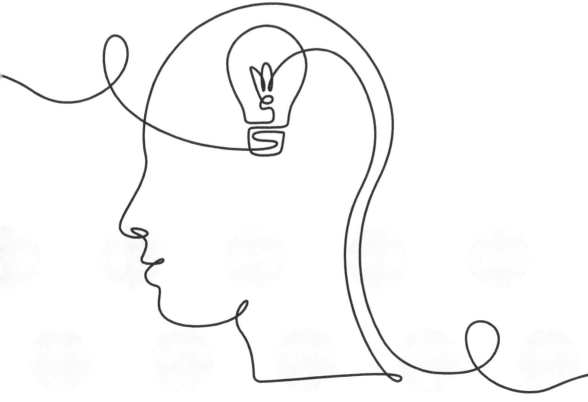

2.6 Speed Dating

In pairs, students are **given two minutes** to ask each other one or more questions. At the end of the two minutes, a bell or other signal is given, meaning that the students need to move on to another speaking partner. Questions can be provided in advance by the teacher or left for students to think up in the moment. Speed dating can be used as an **ice breaker** (see entry 2.4), giving students some time to speak to, and learn something about, each of their new classmates.

For young students a different name for the activity might be needed (such as 'Speed Talking' or similar), in order to avoid students feeling embarrassed or giggling (to distraction) over its name.

2.7 The Plenary

Typically (but not always) taking place towards the end of the lesson, a plenary is intended to help students consolidate and reflect on their learning, and help identify misconceptions and what they do not yet understand. Plenary activities therefore serve to help the teacher formatively assess students' learning, and as such the information gained can feed into subsequent lesson planning. Plenaries may also extend or broaden knowledge as further connections are made between concepts and ideas. Also see plenary dice (2.8) and exit slips (2.9).

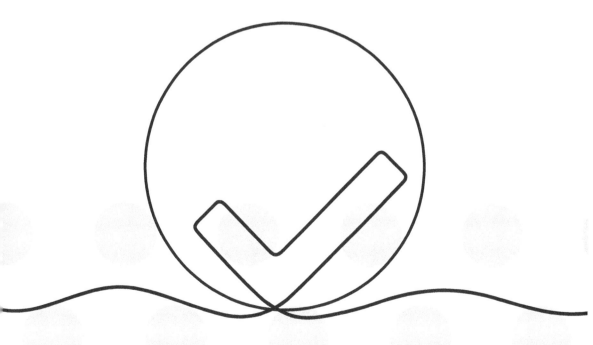

2.8 Plenary Dice

Students roll a **large dice** that has on each face different (generic) **questions** or **instructions** aimed at stimulating **reflection** and **discussion** relating to the lesson. Example instructions and questions include:

- describe two things you learned today;
- say three key words from today's lesson;
- what question do you have about today's lesson topic?
- what more do you want to learn about today's topic?

Discussion can take place in **pairs** or **larger groups**.

2.9 Exit Slips

Students are given a few minutes near the end of class to answer (in writing) a **question** posed by the teacher, relating to the learning content covered in the lesson. Alternatively, an exit slip might include some **sentence starters** which help the students write about the lesson, such as: 'Today I learned about ...' and 'I'm still not clear about ...' The teacher can then **assess** learning through the responses and use this to inform the planning of following lessons. Exit slips can encourage students to **reflect** on their learning and apply their **critical thinking**. They also give quieter students a different opportunity to communicate their thoughts and feelings about the lesson.

Chapter 3

Speaking and Listening

3.1 Think–Pair–Share

The following steps are followed:

- students are given thinking time to **individually** consider a question or problem;
- students are then organised into pairs, in order to discuss their answers;
- some students then share their pair's responses with the **whole class**.

Students can choose pairs themselves, or the teacher might choose pairs in order to ensure students **get to know** new people and hear **new perspectives**. As well as giving students an explicit opportunity to think and formulate their own responses to a question or problem, this activity encourages individuals to consider the (potentially different) responses of others.

3.2 Role-play

One or more students act out an **imagined situation**, in order to practise a particular interaction or skill. Often used in language learning (for
example, at the shops), role-plays can be **scripted** or **unscripted**, the
latter requiring some improvisation (also see **improv**, entry 3.9). As well
as students using their voices, other forms of communication can be
rehearsed, such as **facial expressions** and **gestures**. Role-plays can also
be used to practise trouble-shooting and encourage empathy. Also see
mini dramas (entry 3.8).

It is important to be aware that some students may not feel comfortable
performing or acting out a situation, particularly with an audience. In such
instances an option is to role-play in pairs, with no audience.

3.3 Four Corners

A question or statement is presented, with **four** possible answers displayed in each **corner** of the room. Students **stand** by the answer that most corresponds to their current response relating to the question. To enable more nuanced answers, students can also position themselves **between** two or more answers if they feel their response is somewhere in the middle of these answers. The class **discusses** the responses and students are then given an opportunity to **move** to a different answer if they wish, in light of this discussion. The four corners activity gives students practice in **articulating arguments**, **persuasion**, considering the opinions of others and **critical thinking**.

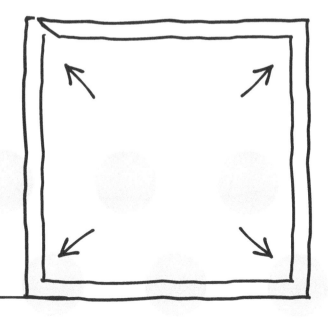

3.4 Diamond 9

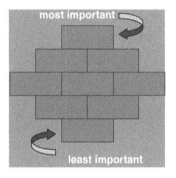

In small groups, students discuss nine different **ideas**, **concepts** or **statements**, each presented on a different card. The group then places each idea on a space on the diamond so they are arranged from **most to least important** (or relevant). Once all cards are placed on the diamond, a spokesperson from each group may be asked to talk though and **justify** their group's card arrangement to the rest of the class. The diamond 9 activity enables students to **evaluate** and **prioritise** ideas and **negotiate**, through working together, to find a consensus.

most important

least important

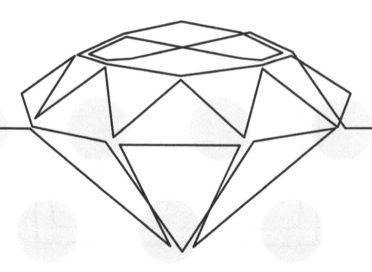

3.5 Debate

Students are divided into (typically) two teams. The teacher introduces a statement (or 'motion') relating to a topic. One team argues **in favour** of the motion while the other team speaks **against** the motion. Before the debate starts, teams may first be given **time to plan** their arguments. The person chairing the debate, usually the teacher, needs to enable speakers to talk without interruption, and give quieter or less confident students opportunities to express their arguments during the debate. Debates can help students develop and rehearse speaking skills and critical thinking. Debates can also involve more than two teams. Debates can take other formats too: see **shrink debate** (3.6) and **balloon debate** (3.7).

3.6 Shrink Debate

This form of debate involves several starting teams, each of which represent a given position on a topic (such as, for example, how to best address climate change). Each team first argues in favour of their position. At the end of a timeframe specified by the teacher, the debate **pauses** and students can then **switch** to any team representing the position they feel is strongest or most agree with. At this point any team left with **no members** is dissolved and no longer represented in the debate. This process can be repeated several times until either time **runs out** or there remains only one or two teams with the most popular positions on the topic. Shrink debates give students **agency** to **reflect** on and change their minds in light of new information.

3.7 Balloon Debate

A group of students imagine a **damaged hot air balloon** losing altitude and holding several passengers. The only way to avoid crashing to the ground will be to **throw out one** or more passengers. Each debater represents a passenger with one or more specific characteristics (such as being very young, or famous, or being a brain surgeon) and has to argue their case as to why they should not be thrown out of the balloon. At the end of the debating period, the **audience** (the rest of the students in class listening to the debate) **vote** on who should be jettisoned from the balloon.

3.8 Mini Drama

A group of students are given a **scenario** and allocated **characters**. The students act out the scene with **scripted** or **improvised** dialogue and movement (for the latter, also see **improv**, entry 3.9). Mini dramas can help individuals reflect on intonation, volume and stress in their spoken communication. This activity also encourages students to empathise and understand the motivations of the characters they are playing. Mini dramas may be particularly useful in language, history and drama classes.

3.9 Improv

Activities that involve students (and sometimes the teacher) participating in spontaneous **speech** and **unplanned** actions, as a particular character and/or in a scenario relating to a topic. Improvisation allows students to apply their creative thinking and communication skills, and to think on their feet. Also see **mini drama** (3.8) and **role-play** (3.2).

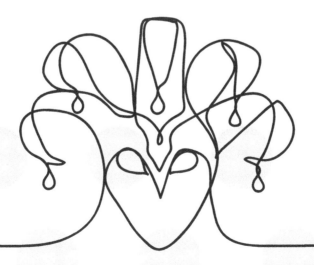

3.10 Storytelling

One or more **students** convey an existing or improvised story to class-mates using words, facial expressions, gestures and (optionally) images. Alternatively, **the teacher** may tell a story to communicate learning content to students in a **memorable way**. In either case, students listen to the speaker and may discuss the story at the end.

For younger students, the group may sit together at the front of class to listen to the story. Storytelling enables students to rehearse (public) speaking and listening skills, and can help them acquire and use new vocabulary.

3.11 Show and Tell

Each student brings an **object from home** to show and discuss with their classmates. There may be a **theme** to the objects, such as something relating to the lesson topic, or an object of a particular colour or shape. Other students may comment or ask questions to the speaker at the end. Mostly used in early years and primary education, 'show and tell' gives students early experiences of presenting and public speaking. Also see **presentation** (3.12) and **realia** (1.4).

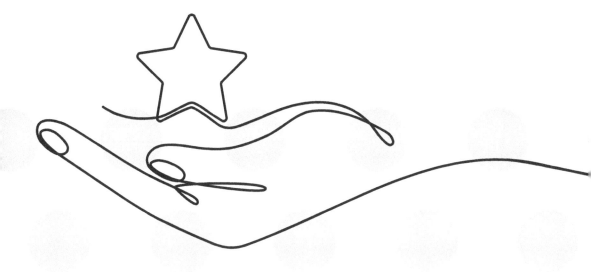

3.12 Presentation

Usually standing at the front of class, one or more students verbally convey information to their classmates, often with the use of **visual aids** such as PowerPoint or Prezi. What is presented might be a **summary** of their learning on a topic, their **project work**, or the presentation of an **argument**. Following the presentation, the rest of the group may **ask questions** to the presenter(s) relating to what has been said. Nervous students may prefer to present from their own desk or sitting down. Alternatively, presentations could be given to smaller groups of students or in other situations, such as at an assembly or to guests.

3.13 Fishbowl

Some students sit in a **circle** and discuss a **specific issue**, while the rest of the class **stand outside** the circle and **listen** to the contributions of the speaking group, **without interrupting**. After a period of time some different students in the group sit and take up the role of speakers. At the end there is a **debrief** of the discussion, enabling **reflection** of what was discussed and the process itself. Fishbowl discussions can help students practise turn-taking and listening to others. Also see **Socratic circles** (3.14).

3.14 Socratic Circles

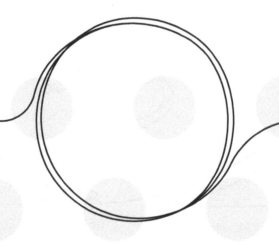

With students in two concentric circles, the inner circle discusses **a text**, with the other circle listening, then (after) giving **feedback** on the discussion. The circles can then **swap** roles. The teacher operates as a **facilitator**, choosing the text, **guiding** the conversation and reflecting on the activity. Discussions are driven through asking **questions**. Note the similarities and differences (in focus) with **fishbowl** discussions (entry 3.13).

3.15 Circle Process

A process to structure dialogue in which each participant has, **in turn**, an opportunity to respond to the teacher's questions, **without interruption** from others. A 'check-in' question may be used at the start for relationship building and to help participants get used to this format. Students are **not required** to speak during their turn, should they not have any additional thoughts or ideas to what has already been said: in these instances participants can simply state their agreement, or their desire to pass to the next person.

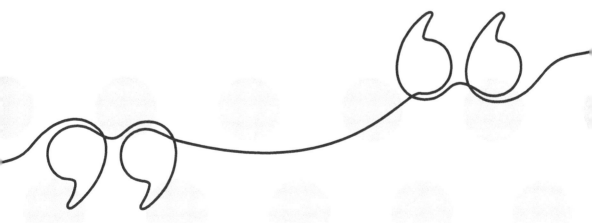

3.16 Circle Time

Students and (often) the teacher sit together in a **circle shape** and engage in **activities** and **games** that are intended to facilitate the development of cooperation, self-esteem, self-awareness, trust, problem-solving, and listening skills. Circle time can also help build a supportive and warm learning environment. Examples of circle time activities include:

- singing songs
- reading a story
- sharing ideas
- discussing the day, achievements, news, or feelings
- making something
- playing a game, such as *Simon* Says

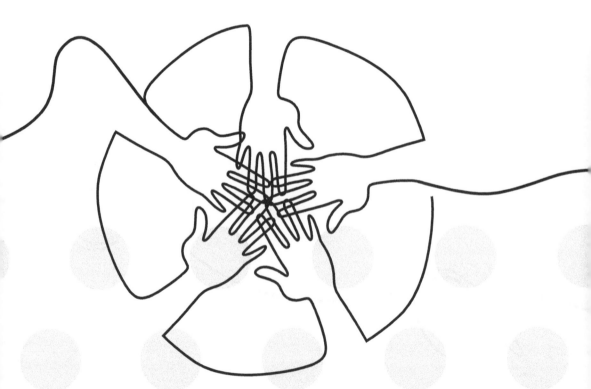

3.17 Buzz Groups

In pairs, students are given a short timeframe to discuss a **question**, **problem**, or **scenario**. Each pair then joins **another** and continues the discussion as a group of four. Buzz groups can work even in large lecture halls, and may be preferred by students who tend not to participate in whole-class discussions. The name derives from the noise generated by all the simultaneous discussions taking place. Also see **think-pair-share** (3.1).

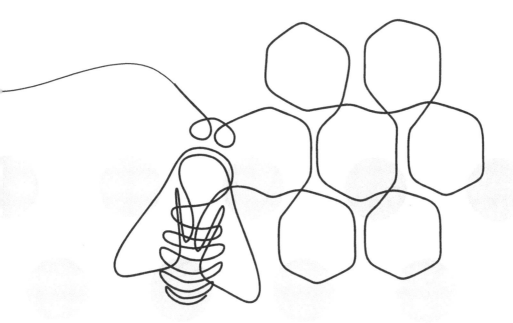

3.18 Feynman Technique

The principle of this technique is that **a person understands** a topic or concept well when they can **explain** it in **simple terms**. Students improve their understanding of concepts and topics through the following process:

1. write down everything they know about a particular concept;
2. explain the concept in simple terms (verbally or in writing), as if teaching a child. This involves using their own language rather than technical jargon;
3. identify what they found most difficult to explain and gaps in their own understanding, and study these aspects further;
4. simplify and otherwise amend their explanation, using analogies to help where possible.

Once the first step is completed, the others can be repeated in a loop, as necessary.

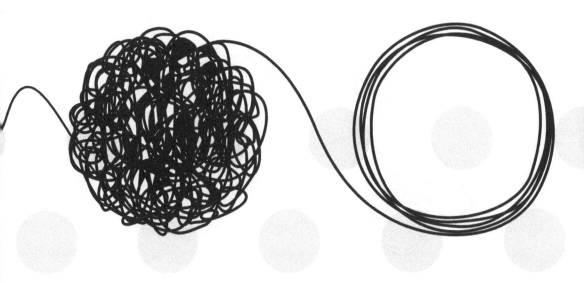

3.19 Graffiti Wall

A space (usually comprising one or more sheets of poster paper pinned to a wall) where students can **share** their thoughts and ideas relating to a **question**, **problem** or **scenario**. This can lead to a **group** discussion based on what students have written and drawn. **Online** graffiti walls can also be used, using **Padlet** or **Mural**, for instance (see **online activities 1**, entry 4.12).

3.20 Court Trial

One student plays the role of the 'accused': a historical or current figure accused of a specified crime, such as a president, monarch, war general, or business owner. The judge and jurors are also chosen, as are lawyers for the defence and prosecution. There may also be students who play the part of witnesses to the crime. The teacher will need to ensure that the students understand the purpose of each of these roles. The classroom may also be arranged in a courtroom-type layout.

In turn, the lawyers question the accused and any witnesses. After, the jurors give their **verdict** as to whether the accused person should be found guilty or acquitted of the crime. Should the accused be found guilty, the judge issues what they determine to be an appropriate punishment. The court trial enables students to practise public speaking, critical thinking and decision-making. It also enables students to recall their understandings of a person or event. Also see **role-play** (3.2) and **improv** (3.9).

3.21 Drilling

Primarily focused on oral skills, drilling involves the teacher saying a word, followed by one or more students **repeating aloud** the same word several times. This process can help students improve pronunciation and memorise words and set phrases. **Whispering** or **shouting** drills can serve to quieten or bring alive a class.

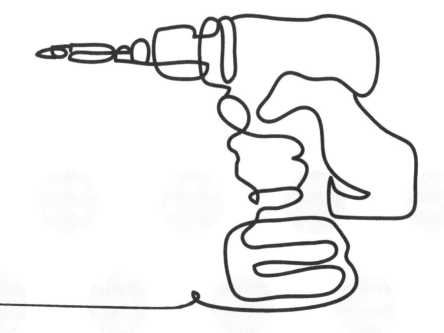

3.22 Shipwrecked

The scenario is introduced that some unfortunate sailors have been ship-wrecked on an island. Working **in small groups**, students are given a list of **materials** they have access to and a period of time (perhaps 30 minutes) to decide how they will use these materials to **survive** on the island and (optionally) **attempt an escape** off the island. The teacher may give a list of items that need to be created, such as a water container, shelter, or a make-shift life-raft. This activity uses students' problem solving, lateral thinking and communication skills.

3.23 Mingle

Mingle activities are **flexible** in purpose and can constitute an **ice breaker** (see entry 2.4), or enable a discussion or survey. Students move around the class, find a partner and ask one or more questions or initiate conversations. The questions can be provided by the teacher or created by the students. Once finished, each student finds a new partner and repeats the process.

For discussions, questions on card or paper (initially provided by the teacher) might be **exchanged** between students after each conversation. For surveys, students keep their set of questions and may note the responses of each student (possibly for later analysis). Extra impetus can be provided by giving a shorter time frame for the activity, or requiring a minimum number of responses to be recorded by each student.

3.24 The Jigsaw

Students are put into 'home' groups of **four to six** (each group needs to be the **same size**). Each student in a home group learns a **different chunk of information** about a topic, as designated by the teacher.

Individuals then leave their home group and gather with people in **other** groups assigned to the **same chunk** of learning as themselves, forming an '**expert group**'. The expert groups then prepare some form of presentation to summarise their chunk of learning.

Students then **return to their home group** and use their presentation (made with the expert group) to explain their chunk of information.

3.25 Demonstrations

A **process** is shown to students either by the teacher, an external expert, or other students. Examples include changing a wheel or making a cake. Those watching can be instructed to **discuss** the process being demonstrated, **predict** outcomes and/or **question** (the process). These features increase student engagement and it has been found (see **Crouch et al., 2004**) that giving students time to make predictions leads to a better understanding of the process or concept being demonstrated.

Crouch, C., Fagen, A.P., J. Callan, P. and Mazur, E. (2004) 'Classroom demonstrations: Learning tools or entertainment?' *American Journal of Physics*, 72(6), pp. 835–838. Available at: https://doi.org/10.1119/1.1707018

3.26 Pose, Pause, Bounce, Pounce

An approach to questioning that facilitates deep thinking and involves the following process:

- **pose** a question to the group;
- **pause** to give students time to think;
- **pounce**: choose a student to answer;
- **bounce** the answer to a different student, who may build on, or add to, the first answer.

Also see **cold calling** (1.10) and **wait time** (1.11).

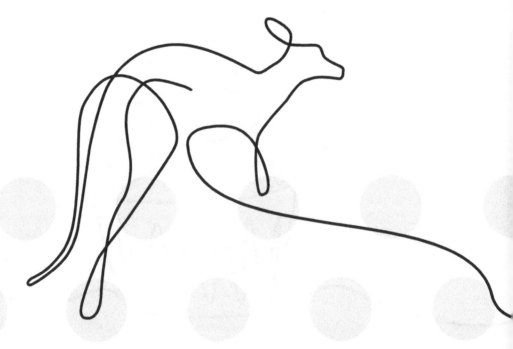

Chapter 4

Reading and Writing

4.1 Graphic Organisers

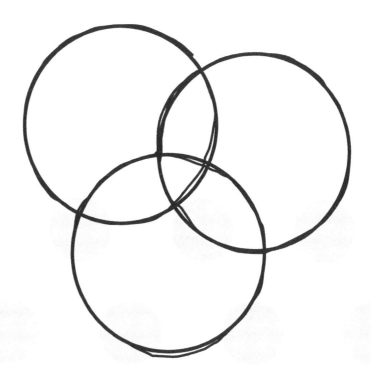

Information is organised visually in a manner corresponding to its purpose, such as a **diagram**, **flow chart**, or **timeline** (for this final example, see entry 4.5). Graphic organisers can be presented to students, or developed by students themselves individually or in groups, to show learning content and relationships between concepts. Graphic organisers can help information recall, and aid learning when there is a **large amount of content** (and possibly **limited time**).

4.2 Chain Notes

Students receive an **open-ended** question on some paper, write their response to the question on the same paper, then pass it on to **another student** for them to add their own response. The papers are passed on several times. Gathering the responses at the end, the teacher can use what is written to **identify patterns** and **gaps** in understanding among the group. Chain notes can also be used to **obtain feedback** regarding the lesson itself. Also see **snowballs** (6.6).

The Super Quick Guide to Learning Activities

4.3 Word Walls

Words are placed on a wall in a learning space as a **reference point** to help students **remember**, **spell** and **use** key topic **words**. Word walls may also be used for frequently used words in general communication. Various **actions** can aid engagement with these words, such as **chanting**, or **clapping** to the syllables while saying them. Walls may also display various other information, such as mathematical **symbols**.

4.4 Sketch Notes

An alternative to standard note-taking (which usually consists of writing verbatim what is heard), sketch notes involve writing down **key words**, **abbreviations** and **symbols** (such as a stick person or light bulb). Words may be emphasised using bold or bubble letters, or by drawing boxes around them. Ideas or concepts can be **linked** with arrows. **Drawings** may also be used to represent ideas, processes and objects. This form of note-taking can help students keep up with and record what is said, and retain new information in a fun, visual way.

4.5 Timelines

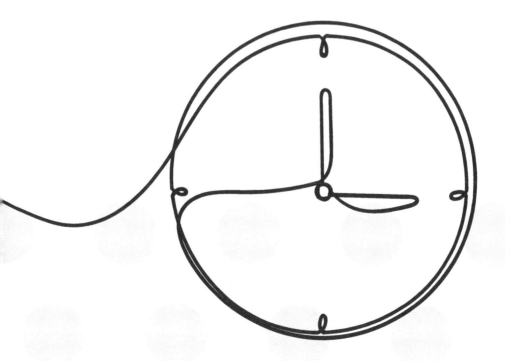

Important events are summarised in **chronological order** along a line that represents a period of time. The start and end of the timeframe is noted at the beginning and end of the line respectively, and key dates are stated alongside each event. Alternatively, the teacher may show a disordered set of events and separate dates, which the students themselves have to **match** and **order** along the timeline. Timelines help clarify the order in which events have taken place and can help students **contextualise** and **connect** one or more events. Timelines are a form of **graphic organiser** (see 4.1).

4.6 Match up

The teacher provides small groups with **two sets** of cards. Each card in one set displays a **key word** relating to a topic. Each card in the second set includes a corresponding **description** or **image**. Students match each key word to its correct description or image. Match up activities can help students to learn and revise vocabulary and key terms. This activity might otherwise involve putting together synonyms or antonyms, lower- and upper-case letters, percentages with decimals, definitions, or problems and solutions.

4.7 Magazine

Groups of around six students create a magazine with a name, front page, and inner pages that may contain articles, reviews, stories, and interviews with imagined or real people. The magazine brings together content that summarises what has been learned in a topic, for example **World War Two** (history), **hobbies** (languages) or **landscapes** (geography).

Groups first agree what the contents will be for their magazine, then each student produces one or more pages of content. The total number of pages produced by groups is contingent on the time given to students for this activity, and the number of students in each group. Creating a magazine can help students practise teamwork and time management, and students have **agency** in how they focus their time during this activity.

4.8 Collage

Images from materials such as newspapers, comics and magazines are cut and pasted together to create a new composite image. Other materials such as feathers or buttons can also be used. Students can create a collage to **convey feelings**, show **information** or tell a **story**. Collages enable students to be **creative** and practise their artistic skills. They can also provide a stimulus for discussion, a presentation, or a debate. Making them can also be lots of fun!

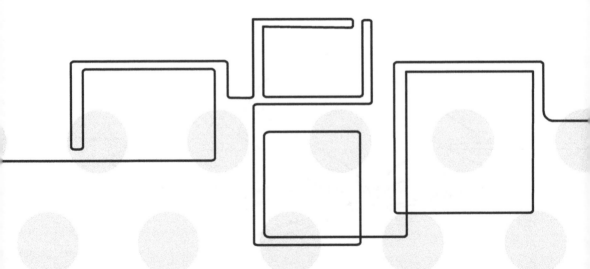

4.9 Police Report

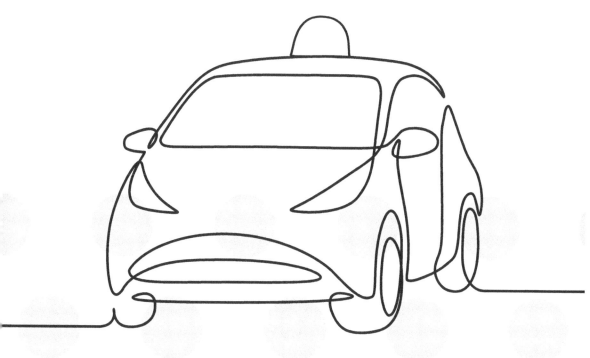

Students recount **an event** through writing a police report. The event may be an imagined or historical crime. A **template** may be provided by the teacher that includes fields for specific information, such as the date, location, people involved, and a description of what happened. Police reports enable students to practise different **verb tenses** (such as the past simple), write with **clarity**, detail, and in **chronological** order. Also see **writing frame** (entry 1.13).

4.10 Co-writing

Students work in pairs to draft a piece of written work. Co-writing can take place **online** – for example, on Microsoft OneDrive – where documents can be edited by more than one person at the same time (synchronously) or at different times (asynchronously). Alternatively, with pens and paper, one student writes while the other contributes (verbal) input as to the structure, tone and words written. These roles can be periodically swapped. Pairs might write an essay, report, a process, or a guide. Co-writing enables students to practise **collaboration** and **negotiation.**

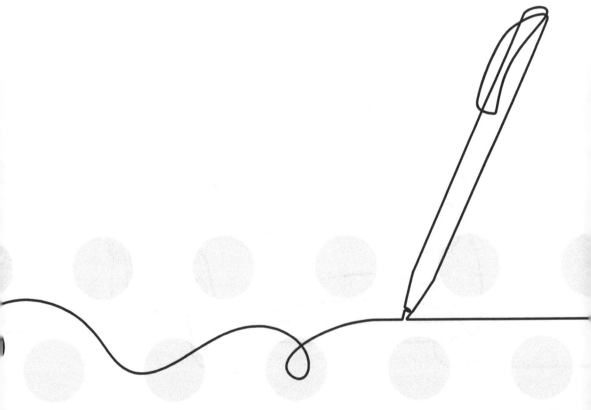

4.11 Book Review

Students write a review of a book they have read. The review may be required to contain certain content, such as comments relating to the main characters, storyline, writing style and an opinion about the book. For non-fiction books this may include giving headlines about main learning points, arguments, processes or concepts. A **writing frame** (see 1.13) may be provided to help structure the review. Reviews can also be presented verbally, enabling discussion about the book. Book reviews give opportunities for students to express **opinions** and consolidate and/or **summarise** learning content.

4.12 Online activities 1

Learning and assessment activities that take place online. For instance:

- **Kahoot, Quizizz** and **Blooket** are interactive sites where students answer **multiple choice questions** in a gamified, competitive way;
- with **Socrative**, students can engage with (often gamified) assessment activities that are then graded;
- on **Padlet** and **Mural**, students can collectively brainstorm ideas and plan projects;
- **DuoLingo** can be used as part of language learning;
- **Prezi** can be used as an alternative to PowerPoint, for students to create and give presentations.

4.13 Online activities 2

Some websites offer **free** and/or **subscription** learning games. For instance, the BBC Bitesize website (www.bbc.co.uk/bitesize) provides a range of learning content and games across subject areas, for primary, secondary, and adult students.

Online activities can also help students develop **computer skills** such as **typing** and **navigating the internet**. Individuals can also research topics and explore learning content available online, using for instance Google Scholar, Wikipedia or AI chat tools, such as Google Bard or ChatGPT. This can take place independently or with others. It is critical, however, that teachers discuss with their students in advance the need to carefully consider the sources and authors of information found online, and that a judgement needs to be made as to the reliability of information in light of these features. Further, teachers need to ensure that the content of websites used by their students are age appropriate.

Also see **blogging** (4.14) and **podcasts** (6.9).

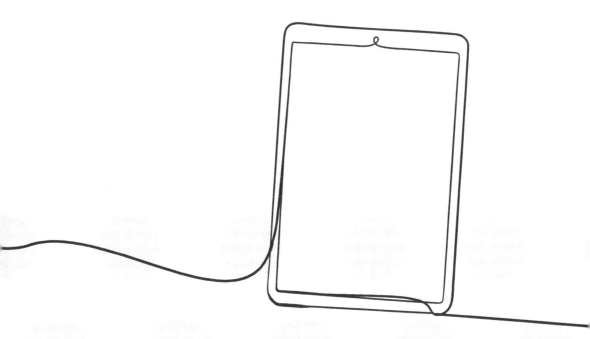

4.14 Blogging

Student blogs: students write online blog entries as a **reflective**, ongoing **journal** of their learning. Other students and the teacher can read and comment on each post, making the blog an online **collaborative tool** for learning.

Teacher blogs: teachers can develop their own blogs to **share** learning materials with students, provide instructions and give advice. Blogs can be open or closed, the former meaning the content is open access for all web users, while the latter requires permission to access content.

4.15 Gap Fill (or 'Cloze')

The teacher hands out or displays a text with words or phrases **missing**. Students write in what they determine to be the missing words. Optionally, the missing words might be provided in a **separate list** for students to choose from. A gap fill activity can enable students to consolidate and demonstrate their understanding of a concept or process. They are also used in **language learning** as a reading comprehension activity or listening exercise. With the latter, a text would comprise song lyrics or lines from a film, with students listening to the song words or film scene and filling in the gaps as they hear the missing words.

4.16 Look, Say, Cover, Write, Check

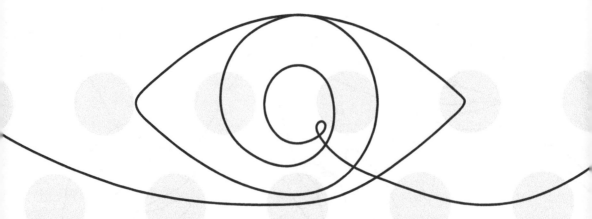

The following process is used to learn the spelling of a new word:

- **look** at the word
- **say** the word out loud
- **cover** the word up
- **write** the word down
- **check** that what has been written matches the correct spelling.

A further stage, '**fix**' is where the student corrects any errors.

4.17 Journalling

The process of keeping a journal to express and record thoughts and reflections relating to learning experiences. Journalling can aid professional learning by capturing **experiences** and enabling reflection and **analysis** of practice. Journalling can also help develop critical thinking and encourage metacognition (Moon, 2006). Also see **blogging** (4.14).

Moon, J.A. (2006) *Learning Journals: A Handbook for Reflective Practice and Professional Development*. 2nd ed. London: Routledge.

4.18 Dictation

With traditional dictation, the teacher reads a text **out loud** as students attempt to **write down verbatim** what is said. As a pair activity, one student is the speaker and the other writes. The reader may read the text (more) **slowly** and/or in **small chunks** with pauses in between, to help the writer. At the end the speaker and the writer evaluate the written text in relation to the original text, and correct errors. Dictation can help with spelling, punctuation and phonological awareness. Also see **running dictation** (4.19) and **Dictogloss** (4.20).

4.19 Running Dictation

Students work in pairs. One student sits and is **the writer**. Their partner jogs or walks to another area in the classroom where a **text** is located, then reads and remembers as much text as possible. They then return and dictate what they remember to their partner, who writes what is said. This process is repeated until either the activity time runs out or the pair finishes writing the whole text. As with traditional **dictation** (entry 4.18), the speaker and the writer then together evaluate the written text in relation to the original, and correct errors.

It is important that, with people moving around the classroom in such a way, teachers and the students ensure in advance that bags and other trip hazards are well out the way. Students need to also remain aware of others moving around them during the activity, to avoid bumping into each other. Popular for language learning, this classroom activity involves **reading**, **writing**, **speaking**, and **listening** in the target language.

4.20 Dictogloss

The teacher **reads a text** to the class several times at normal speed, while students note down **key words** and **phrases** that summarise what is said. Students then use their notes and what they remember to **reconstruct** the text in writing. Dictogloss differs from standard dictation in that students are **not writing** the text **verbatim** as the teacher reads. Also see **dictation** (entry 4.18) **sketch notes** (4.4).

4.21 Pomodoro

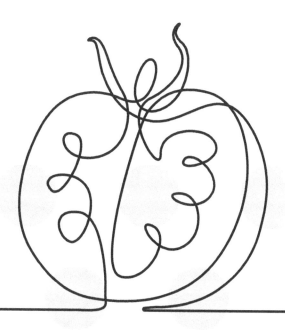

A technique that can be applied to longer writing activities (rather than constituting a learning activity in itself), Pomodoro involves several rounds of a work/break cycle, consisting of around **25 minutes** allocated for the completion of a specific task, followed by a **five-minute** break.

Internal and external **interruptions** are **not allowed** during the work period, such as answering a phone call or talking to others. The Pomodoro technique can therefore help students to **focus** during writing activities both in class and at home. There are various online tools that facilitate timings for the Pomodoro technique. See for example: https://pomofocus.io/ and https://pomodorotimer.online

4.22 Mini Whiteboards

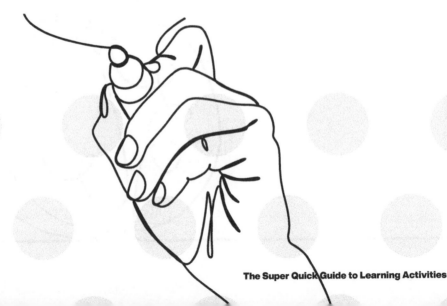

Small handheld whiteboards are given to students on which to **write** or **draw**. Students can hold up the boards to show the teacher and class-mates their **work**, give **feedback**, or show their **answer** to a question. The teacher can quickly **assess** work and students' understanding among the whole group. **Erasable pens** are used and board **cleaners** are also distrib-uted, so the boards can be used for different purposes across consecutive activities. Boards can be used individually, in pairs, or in groups.

4.23 The One-minute Paper

Students have **one** minute to write their response to a **question**, **problem** or **statement** given by the teacher. The teacher can then **collect** responses and **assess** learning. They may also be used to diagnostically assess students' existing knowledge of a topic before it is taught. Responses can be **named** or **anonymous** and **graded** or **ungraded**. One-minute papers can also be completed in **pairs** or **groups**.

4.24 Free Writing

Writing that captures thoughts or ideas at a particular moment in time, in a relaxed and unstructured way. Free writing can be **guided** (when a topic is specified) or **unguided** (where no topic is given). Students may be given a time frame from anything between two and twenty minutes to write down their thoughts.

Free writing is non-editing, meaning the text produced comes fully from the mind of the individual and not from other sources of information. At the end, what is written need not be shared with others, although one or more ideas from the text produced could be used or developed further in subsequent activities.

This form of writing is a **low-stress** activity that enables students to focus on their flow of thoughts and ideas, and not worry about perfect grammar and punctuation.

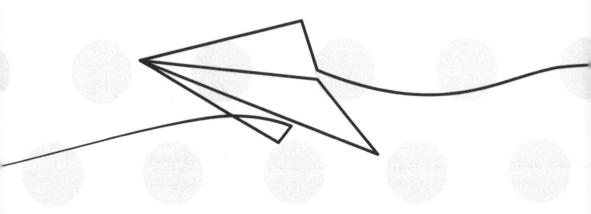

The Super Quick Guide to Learning Activities

4.25 Note to Future Self

Students are firstly encouraged to consider their **goals** and **ambitions**, for five or ten years in the future. Students then write a letter to their future selves, setting out key information such as what job they are doing at that time, where they are living, and what hobbies they are doing. Letters can be written **online** or by **hand**, kept, and opened on the future date. This activity can help individuals to set goals for themselves and think though the steps they need to take to achieve them.

Letters might include sentences such as:

Here in the year _____ I am enjoying my job as a _____ in _____.

I worked hard to get here by studying _____ and making sure I _____.

I got help from _____ along the way.

I've travelled to _____ and seen _____.

I've also learned new skills, such as _____.

4.26 Agony Aunt

Students respond in writing to one or more short letters that summarise problems relating to a topic. Responses typically require giving some form of **advice**. Agony aunt letters are used, for instance, in language learning, where students can practise using **modal verbs**, such as 'you *should* try ...' and 'you *could* ...' . Alternatively, problem letters could be written from historical characters, such as John F. Kennedy, who wants advice relating to the Cuban Missile Crisis. This second example enables students to **reflect** on the situation and options of such figures, and on decisions they later took.

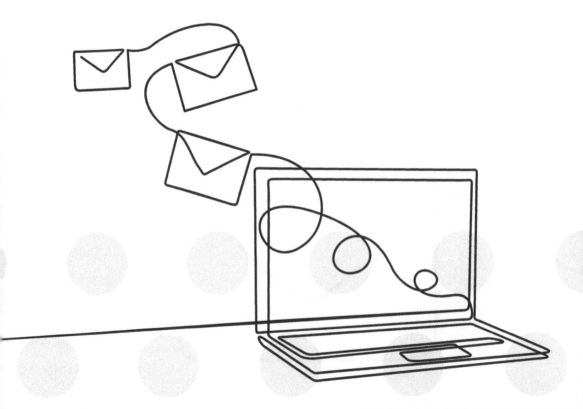

4.27 Silent Debate

A silent debate involves the following process, in which all participants have an equal opportunity to participate and 'voice' their positions through writing:

- a **question** or **problem statement** is presented to the group;
- each student **writes on paper** their response;
- after a short period, the papers are **swapped** around the class and students comment (in writing) on others' positions, adding or building on ideas and communicating agreement or disagreement;
- papers may then be passed around again.

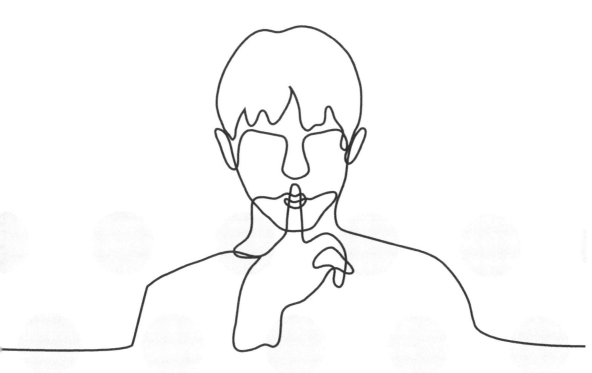

4.28 KWL Charts

KWL is an abbreviation for: **'know'**, **'want to know'** and **'learned'**. Within KWL charts, students summarise their responses to these three aspects in relation to a topic, activating **prior knowledge** and giving students **agency** in determining their own learning goals. First, students complete the 'know' and 'want to know' parts, then finally the third 'learned' part, after reading a text or searching for information relating to the topic. In completing the 'learned' section, students may **correct misconceptions** initially noted under the 'know' section.

KNOW	WHAT TO KNOW	LEARNED
WW1 TOOK PLACE BETWEEN 1914 AND 1918	WHY DID IT START? WHERE DID IT TAKE PLACE?	THE WAR TOOK PLACE MAINLY ACROSS...

Chapter 5

All Communication Skills

5.1 The Washing Line

A line of string is hung above the classroom on which students' work is pegged, like drying clothes on a washing line. Students can then **see** and **celebrate** each other's work. **Examples** of high-quality work might be left on the line during a topic as a reference point for students. Alternatively, the line can be used for **ordering activities**, such as hanging letter cards to form words, or show the alphabet.

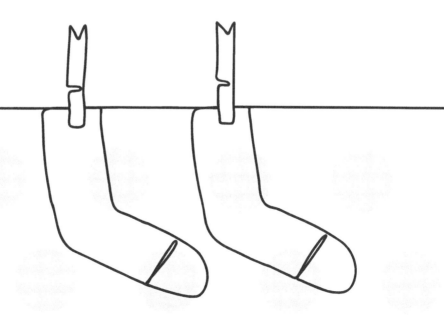

5.2 Learning Stations

Learning stations are different **physical locations** in a classroom. Students rotate through stations in groups, solving a problem or completing a hands-on task at each station, then moving on to the next. Instructions, along with different materials or tools can be provided at each station, such as a computer, paper and pens, books, images, or objects. The teacher specifies how much time is available at each station before groups need to move on.

Learning stations encourage students to engage actively with learning content, collaborate, think critically, and can be used to assess learning. Also see **gallery walks** (5.3) and **marketplace** (5.4).

5.3 Gallery Walks

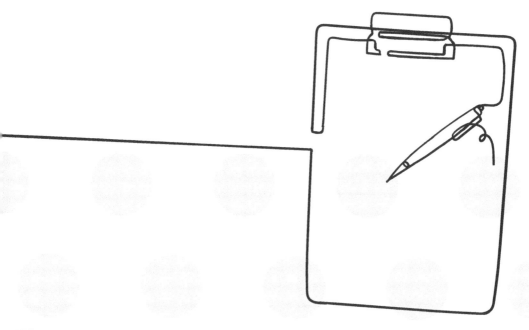

Small groups **rotate** around stations every few minutes. At each station there is a question, problem, poster, or another stimulus (either produced by students or provided by the teacher) that is discussed by the groups. One student in each group may **take notes** of their group's thoughts and ideas, **leaving the notes** at that station. After a specified time period has elapsed, each group moves to the next station and repeats the process, **adding comments** to those recorded by previous groups. Gallery walks give students multiple opportunities to **exchange ideas** and **reflections** about learning content.

5.4 Marketplace

Students are divided into small groups. Each group is provided with a different part of the lesson's learning content and creates a **poster summarising** this content. Students then move around the room, reading the posters made by other groups. One member of each group may remain by their own poster to help explain, or answer questions relating to, their poster. Finally, students then return to their group to share and discuss what they've learned from other posters. Also see **posters** (6.10) and **the jigsaw** (3.24).

5.5 Field Trips

Students **visit** a physical **location** outside their normal learning environment, to facilitate and enhance learning. Groups could visit, for instance: a museum, a library, a zoo, or a beach. **Worksheets** may be provided for students to complete at the location, with completed worksheets later used for subsequent activities, such as writing up and analysing observations, presenting or revising information.

Field trips can **inspire** and **excite** students about their learning, bring the curriculum to life and help individuals **retain** information. Field trips can also, however, require lots of preparation time. It is important that health and safety is considered in relation to all the participants going on the trip.

5.6 Virtual Field Trips

Whereas traditional **field trips** (5.5) involve students visiting places in person, virtual field trips (VFTs) involve an immersive, **simulated visit** to a virtual environment via technologies such as virtual reality headsets, computers, tablets or on a classroom interactive whiteboard. VFTs enable students to explore, observe and test skills within the environment, while being more **time and cost efficient** than in-person field trips. VFTs are not constrained by the practical considerations of getting to 'real' locations and might, therefore, involve visiting for example, historical sites, mountains, factories or parliament buildings – **anywhere** in the world.

5.7 Bingo

Each student is given a card with a **grid of boxes**, each containing a number, word, phrase, definition, or image. No two cards have exactly the same content. Using numbers as an example, the 'caller' (the teacher or a student) reads random numbers, one after the other, from the full list of numbers. On hearing a number that matches one on their card, students mark them as a match. When a student matches an entire row, column, or the whole card, they shout 'Bingo!' and win the game. Bingo can help with the learning of **numbers** or **vocabulary**, and offers an opportunity to rehearse listening skills.

5.8 Freeze Frame

Students are given **30 seconds** to position themselves in a scene as if they were characters in a painting or photo. Scenarios might include a historical battle or a street in Victorian London. The teacher could allocate roles, or the students could decide themselves who they will be in the frame. Once the group freezes in place, the teacher then moves around the group, perhaps with a pretend microphone, asking each student who they are, and what they are doing, thinking, feeling or saying.

The freeze frame stimulates **collaboration**, **communication** and **empathy**, and can be spontaneous or planned in advance. This activity could lead to a subsequent task where students write about the character and their circumstances, perhaps in the form of a diary or journal entry. Also see **improv** (3.9) and **mini drama** (3.8).

5.9 The Lecture

A teacher, student, or an invited speaker **introduces**, **explains**, **evaluates** and/or **critiques** learning content to an audience of students. The students listen, take notes (also see **sketch notes**, 4.4) and may ask questions. A common activity with large student cohorts in higher education, the principal aim is information **transmission** from the speaker to the audience. Greater student involvement can be introduced through, for example, the use of **buzz groups** (see entry 3.17).

5.10 Genius Hour

Dedicated classroom time is allocated for (inquiry) projects that **address questions** developed by students themselves. Students can explore topics independently or work in groups in a collaborative inquiry.

This approach **deviates** from prescribed curricula and recognises **students' voices** and interests. Despite its name, the time allocated for this activity could vary from a few minutes a day to 10 or 20 per cent of class time.

5.11 Research Project

Topic-related research questions are devised by the teacher, students, or both. Students then use one or more research **methods** (such as a survey, interviews, or experiments) to gather data for analysis, and address the research questions. Students can write up their findings as a report, essay, on a poster (see entry 6.10), or as part of a **presentation** (see entry 3.12). Through conducting research projects, students can develop various skills and knowledge, such as **problem solving**, **data analysis**, time management, **research methods** and independent working.

5.12 Board Games

Playing board games can help students practise **decision-making**, applying **strategies**, **predicting** the strategies of others, **negotiating** and other skills. Scrabble or Boggle might be played to practise **spelling**, while Guess Who enables language students to practise forming, asking and answering **questions**.

Board games can be a fun and engaging classroom learning activity, although the rules and purpose of games in relation to learning first need to be understood by students. Students can also design their own board games, through making questions and/or writing actions into a grid of squares.

5.13 Be The Teacher

Students carry out activities that are traditionally done by the teacher, such as **explain a concept** at the front of class, **demonstrate** a process in a lab, or **correct** some written work. Giving students opportunities to 'be the teacher' in these ways can help them **articulate** and **consolidate** their own understandings of the learning content and promote their sense of ownership of the topic or subject. Also see the **Feynman technique** (entry 3.18).

5.14 Student-generated Questions

Students write questions relating to a topic, concept or process, which **other students** answer. Questions can either be:

- handed to the teacher who then reads them to the group;
- put up on walls for written responses; or
- in pairs or small groups students can ask each other their questions.

Student-generated questions can help students **deepen their understanding** and identify **critical information** in learning content. Particularly salient to language classes, question structures are also practised.

5.15 Hot Seat

A randomly selected student sits at the front of class. The teacher and other students question this student on the current topic for a short period of time, such as one or two minutes. When the time has elapsed, another student is chosen to take up the Hot Seat.

In subjects such as politics or history, the person in the seat might assume the role of a prominent figure, such as a prime minister, and address questions relating to their position and/or decisions the figure has made. In a class where business or economics is being studied, students might play the role of a manager or CEO.

This activity can help **motivate** students **to prepare** for class and engage in discussion. Students who feel uncomfortable being in the chair could have the role of asking questions, rather than taking a turn in the Hot Seat.

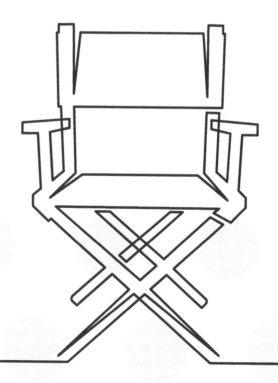

5.16 Blob Tree©

Students consider which character (or characters) in the **Blob Tree** they **most relate** to in reference to a situation, topic, a particular day, or more generally. The **Blob Tree** can help individuals to identify their **feelings** and provide a basis for **reflection** or **discussion**.

This visual representation of feelings through the use of simple characters is the idea and work of **Ian Long** and **Pip Wilson**, who have created a range of 'Blob' books, each centred on different themes, such as relationships, resilience and mindfulness. To discover more about Blob Tree, visit their website at https://www.blobtree.com

5.17 Choice Boards

Students **choose** which activities they will do to learn or practise the **intended content**, from a range (presented in boxes as instructions). Giving students choice and agency in this way can improve **motivation** and **engagement** in learning. Choice boards are also a straightforward way to involve differentiated instruction.

CHOICE BOARDS		
WRITE A POEM ABOUT...	LIST...	DRAW A CHARACTER IN...
LABEL AN IMAGE OF...	DRAW A DIAGRAM OF...	WRITE A LETTER TO...
WRITE A SUMMARY ABOUT...	BRAINSTORM...	ANNOTATE...

5.18 Go Find

The teacher places information **around the class walls** on posters or cards. Students **circulate** and find the information they need to answer questions or gather **key facts** relating to a topic. Movement around the room could be managed in groups, or free flow in nature, meaning students can move around individually at their own pace. 'Go Find' gives students an opportunity to stretch their legs while completing a question-and-answer activity. Also see **Rat Race** (5.19).

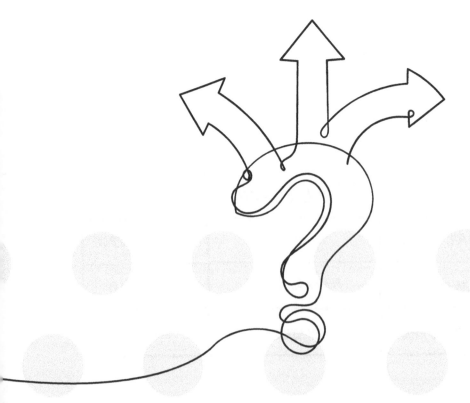

5.19 Rat Race

In pairs or small groups, students are given a text such as a report, article or textbook. Once the activity starts, a student from each pair or group **runs to the teacher** at the front of the class and receives a question card. The student then returns to their group, who together look for the answer in the text. A student from the group then goes back to the teacher, states their answer and, if correct, receives the next question card for their group to answer.

The teacher could make the fastest team to finish every question the winner, although this is optional. Rat race can inject energy and a competitive element into the classroom. As with a **running dictation** (see 4.19), it is important that with people moving around the classroom in such a way, teachers and the students need to ensure in advance that bags and other trip hazards are well out the way. Students need to also remain aware of others moving around them during the activity to avoid bumping into each other. Also see **go find** (5.18).

5.20 Scavenger Hunt

Typically completed in teams, students carry out a set of tasks within a given timeframe. This may involve, for instance, **finding** particular **objects** or some specific information. Scavenger hunts can take place in differing contexts, such as within a classroom, around a playground or across a university campus. The purpose of this last example can also be to help new students get to know their campus.

Hunts can also take place online, with students seeking certain topic-related data. See **online activities 2** (4.13) for a summary of what needs to be considered by students when searching for information online. Scavenger hunts can help students learn and explore in an energetic, hands-on way.

5.21 Experiments

Practical experiments **test predictions** and/or **collect data** that address research questions.

The following are two examples of experiments in the classroom (lab) environment:

- a particular food is left in a container in order to observe its decomposition over time.
- chemicals can be combined in test tubes to observe reactions.

At home, students might combine ingredients to make homemade slime. It has been argued that learning through experiments is **enhanced** when students **write a report** following them (see Cartwright and Stepanova, 2012).

Cartwright, E. and Stepanova, A. (2012) 'What do students learn from a classroom experiment: not much, unless they write a report on it', *Journal of Economic Education*, 43(1), pp. 48–57. Available at: 10.1080/00220485.2012.535710

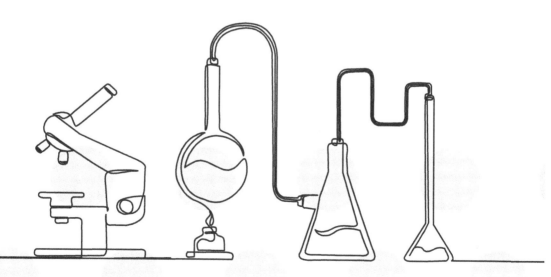

5.22 Case Study

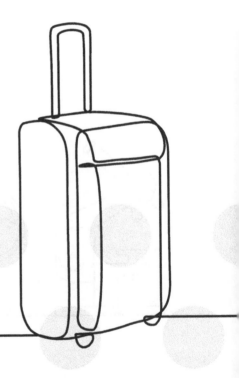

Students are presented with information relating to a real-world **situation**, **event** or **person**, through text, data sets, images or video footage. Individually or in groups, students then analyse the information to develop answers or recommendations to open questions, such as: 'in this scenario, what is the best course of action ...?' Class discussions relating to the case may also follow. Case studies can enable students to apply their under-standings, critical thinking and problem solving to real-world scenarios and contexts.

Chapter 6

Revision and Assessing Learning

6.1 Traffic Lights

An activity that facilitates **self-assessment**, where students each show one of **three coloured cards** to communicate to the teacher their current level of understanding:

- the **green** card means the student feels they understand the learning content well;
- the **yellow** card means they partly understand;
- the **red** card communicates that the student doesn't currently understand the learning content.

The chosen card can be held up, or placed on the desk if students feel uncomfortable doing the former. This form of assessment can help the teacher determine whether part or all the current topic needs to be revisited, or whether to move on to the next topic.

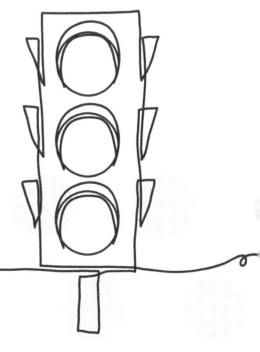

6.2 Elevator Pitch

Students **verbally summarise** to classmates and/or the teacher new knowledge, an idea, or an argument. Each student has between one and three minutes to communicate this information. The teacher may give their group time in advance to write their pitch, and students can also practise their pitches in pairs, before pitching to the whole group. Following each pitch there may be an opportunity for other students or the teacher to offer feedback.

The elevator pitch provides an opportunity for students to practise succinctly communicating ideas. Also see **presentations** (3.12) and the **Feynman technique** (3.18).

6.3 Dominos

Students are given small cards (or they can cut out their own), each with two blank spaces. In pairs, students **write** a **key word** relating to a topic in each blank space. Next, the cards are shared between the partners, who then take turns to lay a card (or domino) on the table, as in the game of dominos. A key word can only be placed next to another if there is some thematic **connection between adjacent words**, which the student laying the card explains if needed. The image on this page illustrates this activity in relation to World War Two. Dominos can form a consolidation or revision activity with a **game element**.

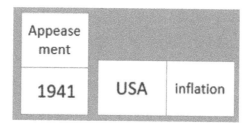

Appease ment		
1941	USA	inflation

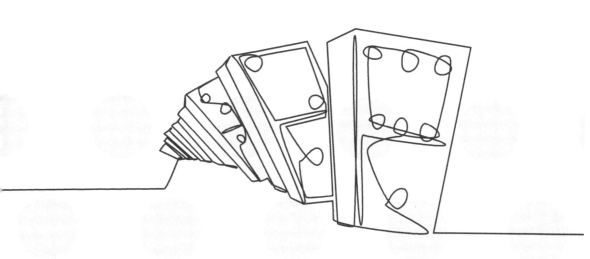

6.4 Pub Quiz

Students are split into groups of four or more, and each group decides on a team name. The teams agree on, and write down, their answer to one or more rounds of questions given by the **quizmaster** (usually the teacher). At the end, each correct answer is given a point, and the team with the most points wins. The Pub Quiz is a collaborative, engaging and fun formative assessment activity.

Teachers can use online tools to ask questions for the pub quiz activity, such as Kahoot or Quizizz. Also see **online activities 1 (4.12)**.

6.5 Peer Marking

Two students mark a piece of each other's work. This means giving their **judgements** (and possibly **grading**) the work of their partner against specific **criteria** provided by the teacher. Peer marking encourages students to think carefully about assessment criteria, and involves the **evaluation** and **reflection** of work.

Some students may feel uncomfortable marking peers' work. This can be addressed to some degree by **anonymising** both the person whose work it is, and who marked it. In this scenario, the teacher collects and hands out work among students, both to mark and return.

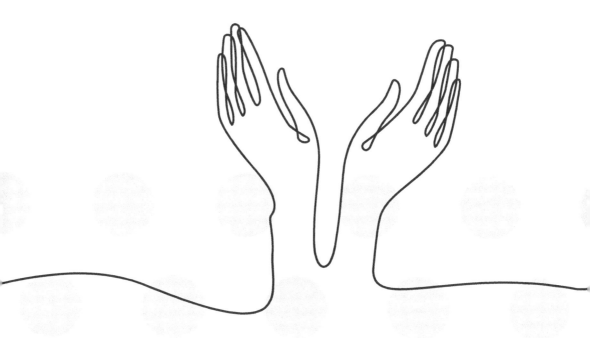

6.6 Snowballs

The following process is followed in the snowball activity:

1. Students firstly **write an answer** to a question given to them on some paper by the teacher.
2. They then **screw up the paper** into a ball.
3. On the count of three, the group then **throw** the papers up in the air, so they fall like snowballs.
4. Students **pick up** a snowball that lands near them and **open it** up. They then add to, correct, or improve the answer they find written on the paper by the previous student.

These steps can be repeated one or more times. Another formulation is where students write a **topic-related question** on paper themselves and throw up the snowballs in the same way, with recipients answering the questions written by their fellow students. Also see **silent debate** (4.27).

6.7 Gameshows

A **revision** or **assessment** activity in the form of a TV gameshow, such as *Who Wants To Be A Millionaire?*, *Just a Minute*, *Jeopardy*, or *Call My Bluff*. The regular rules of the gameshow are followed as much as possible, with the teacher (usually) as quizmaster and students being contestants.

For instance, with *Just a Minute*, one student attempts to talk for **one minute** about a topic without **hesitation**, **repetition**, or **deviation**. If another student notices any of these in what is being said, they raise their hand to pause the speaker, identify the error, then (if agreed by the quizmaster) take over as the speaker for the rest of the minute. Gameshows could be played in pairs, in groups, or as a whole class. Also see **pub quiz** (6.4).

6.8 Two Stars and a Wish

Completed either by the teacher, a peer, or students themselves, **two aspects** of some work are identified and **praised** (the two 'stars') and one aspect is noted as an **area of development** (the 'wish'). The teacher might provide a **writing frame** (see 1.13) to help students give this form of feedback, which might otherwise be difficult. 'Two stars and a wish' therefore enables students to **reflect** on work both in terms of specific strengths and where improvements can be made.

6.9 Podcasts

Online **video** or **audio episodes** uploaded to a webpage, in which a topic is discussed. Teachers may share existing podcasts or create their own in order to **introduce** or **summarise** learning content.

Students can also create podcasts themselves, to record thoughts and ideas, or demonstrate their understanding. The process of summarising and discussing a topic on a podcast can help students retain new learning content, and enable teachers to assess learning. Also see **blogging** (4.14).

6.10 Posters

Students **summarise** topic information, a process, or a concept on some large paper, which can then be placed on classroom or hallway walls. **Text**, **images**, **diagrams**, and other graphics can be used to show and explain the content.

Online platforms can be used to create posters, such as Visme (visme.co), Canva (canva.com) and Microsoft Publisher. Posters can be made individually or in small groups and used as the visual aid of a **presentation** (3.12) or **marketplace activity** (5.4).

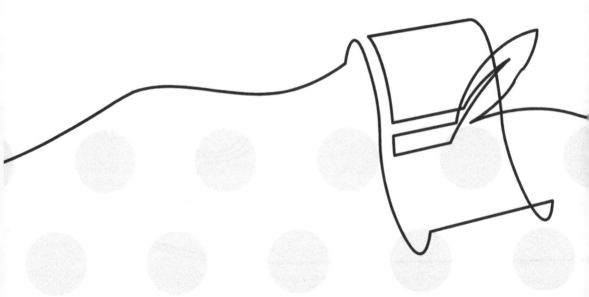

6.11 Brain Dump

Students **write down** everything they can remember relating to a topic. This process can help individuals to **recall** (and help teachers to establish) important information they already know relating to a topic. Brain dumps can be done individually or in groups. Also see **brainstorms** (entry 2.6).

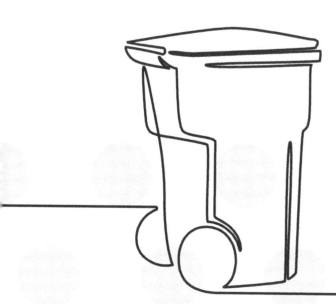

6.12 Low-stakes Testing

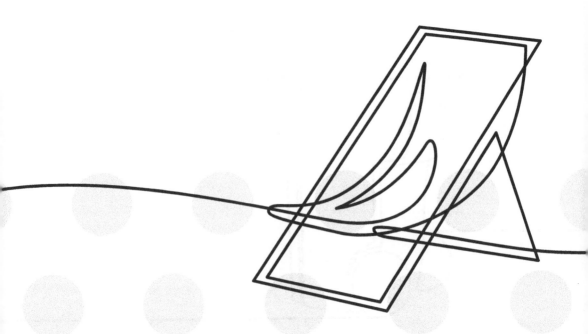

A type of formative **assessment**, such as a **quiz**, that does **not** lead to a 'pass' or 'fail' outcome and therefore tends to result in **low(er)** student **anxiety**. Such testing can both aid knowledge **retention** and enable opportunities for **meaningful feedback**. Also see (and compare) with **summative tests** (page 6.13).

6.13 Summative Test

A **formal** test that takes place **after** a period of instruction, intended to **evaluate** students' learning against standard criteria. Summative tests usually lead to some form of **grading**. Typical formats include, for instance, an end of year **exam**, or end of unit/topic **project**, **portfolio**, **test**, or **assignment**. Also see **low-stakes testing** (entry 6.12).

6.14 Taboo ©

Students work in **groups of four**. One person is the timekeeper, and another is the scorekeeper. The third student is the **'guesser'** and the fourth is the **'clue giver'**. The game involves a pack of cards, with each card displaying a key term and two 'taboo' words.

The following process is observed:

1. The clue giver takes a card from the pack and attempts to verbally **explain the term** to the guesser **without saying** the taboo words, until the guesser says the correct term.
2. The clue giver then picks another card and repeats the process, trying to explain the next key term.
3. The guesser has one minute to guess as many words as possible. After the minute is up, roles are rotated around the group.

Taboo is a fun revision activity to help students practise articulating the meaning of key topic words and terms.

6.15 Top Trumps

Topic-based **template cards** are provided, on which students add numerical information for attributes relating to a person, object, or place. In pairs, students then deal the cards equally, and play Top Trumps as follows:

1. One player reads an attribute of the person, object, or place on the card at the top of their deck, with their partner then reading the corresponding value on their own card. Whichever partner has the **higher** number for that attribute wins their partner's card.
2. Whoever wins the card leads the next round, meaning they choose which attribute is **compared** for the next card in their pack.

Top Trumps is a fun and engaging revision activity that helps students memorise key information. Also see **board games** (5.12).

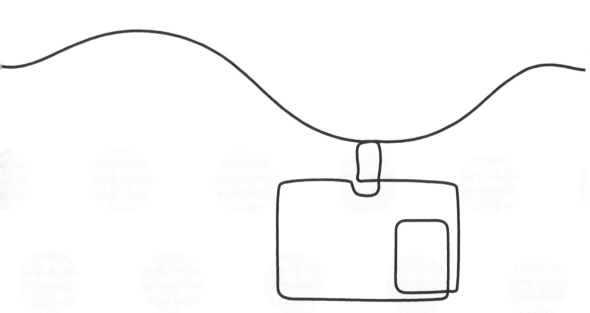

6.16 Quick Quick Quiz

Every student is given a **question card** relating to the topic, which also provides the answer. They must then do the following:

1. Students find a partner and ask their question.
2. If one or both students in the pair **cannot answer** their partner's question, their partner reads the answer and the pair swap cards. They then find another partner.
3. If both students in a pair **correctly answer** each other's question, both keep their card and move on to another partner.

This form of quizzing can be used to revise or consolidate learning, or to introduce new information. It can also inject some energy into a session. Also see **mingle** (3.23).

Index of entries